BROOKLYN'S LUCKY FIN

a blessed adventure by
Jenna Regan

Charleston, SC

www.PalmettoPublishing.com

Brooklyn's Lucky Fin

Copyright © 2020 by Jenna Regan

First Edition

Printed in the United States

ISBN-13: 978-1-64990-523-9

DEDICATION

This book is dedicated to all children born to stand out! Our family adores Brooklyn and we are so proud of her! Her Lucky Fin makes her extra special to us and unique in her own way. We know she was born to help others find self-confidence, beauty within, and acceptance. Always remember that what defines you is who you are at heart!

Brooklyn, we will always be your biggest fans!

Love,

Mommy, Daddy, Harper, Carter & Charlie

I would also like to thank our loving family for their continued support. Brooklyn is one of eight grandchildren and is the seventh grandchild to her Pop and to her loving GiGi in Heaven. She is also the fourth grandchild to her Pop Pop and Grammy. She loves her aunts, uncles and cousins very much and looks forward to making lots of memories with them.

ACKNOWLEDGMENTS

The Lucky Fin Project

Please visit their website **http://www.luckyfinproject.org** to learn more!

"A child being born with a limb difference is not tragic. It's extremely important to show our children how capable & wonderfully made they are. If we treat them as flawed or limited that is who they will believe themselves to be- and that would be the tragedy." -Molly Stapelman, founder.

The Lucky Fin Project is a 501(c)(3) nonprofit organization that exists to raise awareness and celebrate children and individuals born with symbrachydactyly or other limb differences (upper, lower, congenital, and amputee).

What They Do:

- Create a support network for parents across the U.S. and around the world

- Link parents to medical information and resources.

- Provide education on limb differences.

- Host events and financially support efforts for children attend specialized camps and obtain prosthetics.

- Fund other organizations within the limb different community.

10% of each book purchase will be donated to The Lucky Fin Project

On one beautiful spring day with the sun beaming, Brooklyn was on her way to school for the exciting and anticipated Field Day activities. She was determined, full of grace, and fearless. She knew today was a day she wanted to shine with her Lucky Fin.

Just before she closed the door, her mommy shouted, "Keep your head high, don't stop smiling, and remember— the sky is the limit."

Brooklyn smirked, looked back, blew a kiss, and thought, "I know I am strong. My light shines bright, and no one can dim it."

On her walk to school, Brooklyn was excited but started to feel anxious and nervous for Field Day. Her older sister Harper and older brother Carter walked with her to cheer her up. They reminded her that she would do an awesome job today and not to let her difference get in the way.

She knew all of the activities would be challenging, but she kept telling herself that with a good attitude, hard work, and perseverance, she can do anything!

As Brooklyn approached her school, she saw her cousin JoJo, who was in the same grade. "Hi Brooklyn, are you ready for today?" yelled JoJo.

"Yes, I cannot wait! I hope I can do all of the activities with my Lucky Fin," Brooklyn replied.

"Oh, you will. I don't doubt it. You always amaze me with everything you can do!" exclaimed JoJo.

Mrs. Gaffney, the school principal, shouted for all of the students to line up on the black top with their teachers.

"Please remember today is a day for teamwork, cheering others on, and never giving up," she prompted.

The first activity for today would be shooting hoops. Each class lined up at the basketball court line and waited their turn to shoot the ball. The class with the most points would win this competition.

It was Brooklyn's turn on the shooting line. She took shot after shot and never missed one! Her peers stood there in astonishment, and her class took the lead for the shooting hoops matchup.

The second Field Day activity was Monkey Bar races. Brooklyn's class lined up and anxiously awaited their turn. Noah, a boy in Brooklyn's class, turned to her and said, "I don't think you can do this one with your hand." Brooklyn's eyes filled up with tears as she felt defeated and couldn't find the right words to say back to him.

Brooklyn's heart started to race, and her cheeks became blush. She knew this activity was tricky, but suddenly remembered what her daddy had taught her. She recalled that he told her to use her strength on her stronger side to help assist her to get across.

She took a deep breath and took a leap. She looked back at Noah and said, "I can do anything I put my mind to." One by one she soared from bar to bar in record time. Her class applauded her, and she finished with a grin. Noah stood there in disbelief. "Wow, good job Brooklyn! You really can do everything," he exclaimed. Brooklyn smiled and felt very proud of herself.

The final competition of the day had begun — wheelbarrow races. The principal once again signaled for the races to commence and the children started to race. Brooklyn's class was in the lead and needed to win this last feat.

Brooklyn and her partner were on the starting line and he began to push her. She stumbled and had a set-back, but picked herself back up and started to move faster than ever. Her partner yelled, "You got this!"

Brooklyn made it by an inch and they won the race! Her class jumped up and down and shouted with glee!

Pride was written all over Brooklyn's face! She and her classmates were the winners of Field Day!

On the walk home from school, Harper and Carter both gave her a high five and said they were very proud of her!

Brooklyn reflected on the wonderful, victorious day. She realized she learned a lesson about herself. She thought to herself, *If I work hard, I can accomplish hard tasks, and regardless of what anyone thinks, those with good hearts will see me for exactly who I am. I am a hard worker, kind, and am someone who will not let challenges stand in my way. I am ready to conquer the world —no matter what anyone has to say!*

ABOUT THE AUTHOR

Jenna Regan, a certified Elementary Teacher, with a Masters in Curriculum and Instruction, resides in Absecon, New Jersey with her husband Jim, daughters Harper and Brooklyn, son Carter, and her fourth child who is due in August 2020. This is her first children's book and she plans to use this platform to spread awareness about limb differences and acceptance.

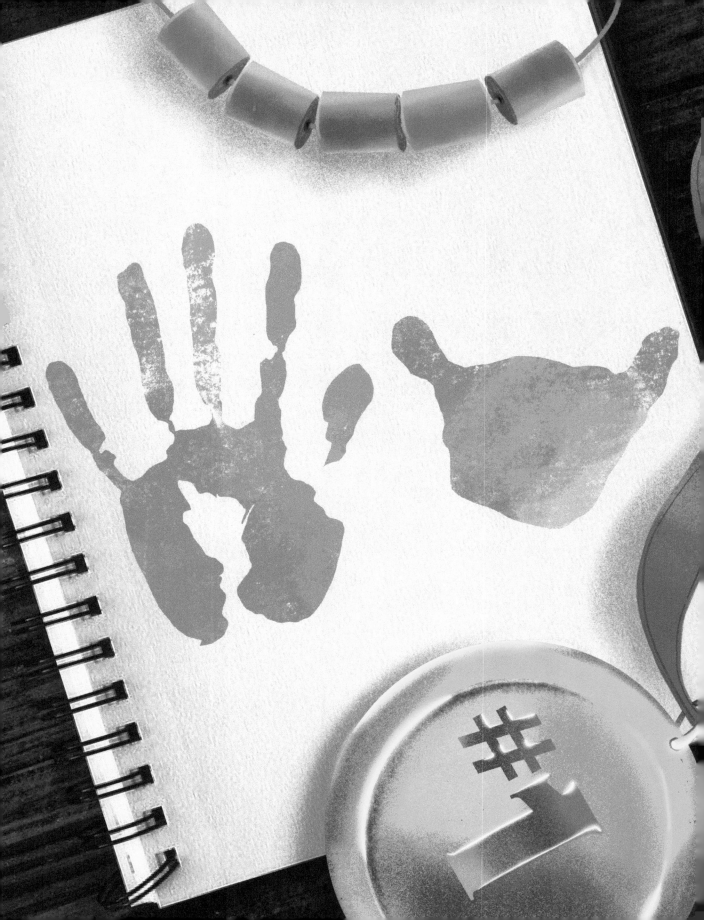

Comprehension Questions to Ask:

1. On the cover page, what do you think Brooklyn's Lucky Fin is?

2. When Brooklyn leaves for school, why do you think she is nervous?

3. What does perseverance mean?

4. What are some adjectives you would use to describe Brooklyn?

5. How do you think Noah made Brooklyn feel?

6. What did Brooklyn learn about herself?

7. What is one thing you learned about someone with a difference?

8. What is the theme of this story?

Additional Activities:

1. Draw a picture of a time you were proud of yourself.

2. Write down something that makes you different.

3. Discuss how Brooklyn's difference is something you can see, but everyone has differences, some you can see and others you can't.

4. Have a kindness circle. Share something kind about someone in your class.

Printed in the USA
CPSIA information can be obtained
at www.ICGtesting.com
LVHW070722261023
761974LV00014B/221